HOTELS L.

Sophie Hannah

HOTELS LIKE HOUSES

To Chantal,
Best wishes,
Sophie Hannah

CARCANET

For Jenny with love

First published in 1996 by
Carcanet Press Limited
402-406 Corn Exchange Buildings
Manchester M4 3BY

A CIP catalogue record for this book
is available from the British Library
ISBN 1 85754 252 5

The publisher acknowledges financial assistance
from the Arts Council of England and North West Arts

Set in 10 pt Palatino by Bryan Williamson, Frome
Printed and bound in England by SRP Ltd, Exeter

Contents

Acknowledgements

Some of the poems in this collection first appeared in the
following publications: *Acumen, The Argotist, As Girls Could Boast*
(Oscars Press, 1994), *The Buzz, Critical Survey, The Dark Horse, The
Frogmore Papers, Gunslingers, The Huddersfield Contemporary Music
Festival Programme 1995, The Interpreter's House, Kent & Sussex
Poetry Society Competition Anthology 1995, London Magazine, The
North, The Observer, Orbis, PN Review, Poetry Review, Prop, The
Secret Garden* (Prospero Press, 1996), *Smiths Knoll, The Spectator,
Stand* and the *Times Literary Supplement.*

'She Can Win Favour' was first broadcast on *The Mark Radcliffe
Show* (BBC Radio One, November 1995), 'Two Hundred and
Sixty-Five Words' on Radio Wales in December 1995, 'His Rising'
on *Stanza* (BBC Radio Four, January 1996), and 'Postcard from a
Travel Snob' on *Postcards* (BBC World Service Radio, February
1996).

Three Hundred Years for Me

He spent last summer in a caravan
With four professors and a Polish priest.
He spent this morning with the Seafood Man
And lunchtime at a window cleaners' feast.

He spent the weekend in a bungalow
Owned by a bloke who used to teach me French.
This evening he'll be at the early show
Of some new film, then on a cold park bench

With ski instructors from the Cairngorm slopes.
He'll spend tomorrow in a parking lot
With a Duke's niece who writes the horoscopes
For women's magazines. Then, when he's got

An hour, maybe half an hour free
I'll make him wait three hundred years for me.

Where is Talcott Parsons Now?

(Talcott Parsons was an American sociologist)

Could a man in your position
Ever love a girl like me?
Would you have to get permission
From the aristocracy?
Just a normal girl, no dowry,
With a house which, at first glance,
Looks like something drawn by Lowry?
Would we ever stand a chance?

Am I utterly deluded
Or could such a love exist?
Would I have to be included
In the Civil Honours List,
Hang about with landed gentry,
Or would access be denied?
Would there be a firm no entry
To all persons from Moss Side?

Are your exes all princesses
Who could spot a pea with ease?
Do they wear designer dresses
And have dinner with MPs?
Are they many times my betters
With their titles, wealth and fame?
Does each one of them have letters
Queueing up beside her name?

Would it be too much to handle?
Would your folks rewrite their wills?
Would it lead, perhaps, to scandal
Or some parliamentary bills?
Would the penalties be hefty?
Will we know until we've tried?
Is the heart a closet lefty
That will not be stratified?

I remember how I hated
Sociology at school
And I've only ever dated
Normal people as a rule.
Masses loving other masses
Maybe never need to learn
That ye olde social class is
Still a relevant concern.

Can mobility be hurried?
Where is Talcott Parsons now
When I need him, when I'm worried?
Do the text books not allow
For a man in your position
Just to have the briefest whirl
(In the Mills & Boon tradition)
With an ordinary girl?

Do I Look Sick?

The gap you leave beside me is unfillable.
I have had just enough of you to care.
I wish your name contained an extra syllable.
Please do not ever shave or cut your hair.

If only there was altogether more of you,
Though some would argue there's already quite a lot.
I'm hoping to deprive the foreign poor of you.
I've no desire to stay at home and write a lot

Nor will I be donating you to charity.
Let's face it – I've become proprietorial.
I don't need someone mystical or taroty
To tell me this weekend is a memorial

To last weekend and to the time I spent with you.
You left too soon and I was in a hurry so
I failed to mention maybe sharing rent with you.
Do I look sick? I eat a lot of curry though.

Each morning is a painful anniversary.
I stank of smoke and scotch but you smelled clean to me.
If I could get a special grant or bursary
I'd fill in forms, explaining what you mean to me.

I asked for nothing at the time. How cool I was,
How casual. I'm sorry for misleading you.
All subsequent events show what a fool I was.
I should have known that I would end up needing you.

I act like I'm some expert on relationships.
Right now I'm waiting for my life to mend a bit,
Eating a bag of Piccadilly Station chips
And writing this. You'll never hear the end of it.

In the Bone Densitometry Room

I could say that my life is my own
When you ask where I've been and with whom
But my voice has the tone
Of a powdery bone
In the bone densitometry room.

I could say there are rats in my throne.
I'm a helium bride with no groom,
Just a motorway cone,
And I crush like a bone
In the bone densitometry room.

It is not what you seek to postpone.
It is not what you wrongly assume.
This erogenous zone
Is as smooth as a bone
In the bone densitometry room.

Are my feelings as commonly known
As a raid on a high-rise in Hulme?
Are they tapping my phone?
Am I really a bone
In the bone densitometry room?

If my cover's already been blown
They can sweep me away with a broom.
When you leave me alone
I'm a shivering bone
In the bone densitometry room.

Neither Home Nor Dry

No need to put your magazine away
If there's an article you want to read;
I could just sit and look at you all day.
Were you about to speak to me? No need.
My minimum is very bare indeed.

I'm happy eating breakfast on my own
Knowing that you are in a room nearby,
Smugly asleep. I'm happy to postpone
Thought and decision, question and reply
For now, since I am neither home nor dry.

You want to stir your drink? I'll fetch a spoon.
I'll wear my heels down looking at the sights
Because you say I should. We're leaving soon.
I watch the pattern form. I may have rights
But no time has been set aside for fights.

Soon I'll be in my favourite service station
(Well-named, because it is a welcome break),
Eating a slice of sickly *Fudge Temptation*
As usual. With such a lot at stake
It's comforting to recognise a cake.

Hotels like Houses

She is the one who takes a shine
to ceilings and to floors,
whose eye finds room for every line
scratched on the wardrobe doors.

She thinks in terms of thick red rope
around the bed, a plaque
above the hardened bathroom soap.
He's always first to pack.

If their affair has awkward spells,
what's bound to cause the rows is
that he treats houses like hotels
and she, hotels like houses.

From A to B (when B is miles from A)

He sold his car the day before they met
Not knowing she would live so far away.
Perhaps he would have sold it anyway
If he was broke, or if his mind was set

On doing so, but it is hard to get
From A to B when B is miles from A.
He sold his car the day before they met
Not knowing she would live so far away –

A fact she won't forgive and can't forget.
Ideally, she'd see him every day.
Whether he feels the same, it's hard to say.

People with cars can have affairs, no sweat.
He sold his car the day before they met,
Not knowing she would live so far away.

Do Detached Houses Want to be Detached?

Do detached houses want to be detached
Or would they rather get beyond their gates
And team up with a dozen box-like mates,
Be smaller, cheaper homes on rough estates
Where it's not safe to walk, where bags are snatched?

Are they quite happy self-contained and proud
Or would they like to slide along the road
(New meaning to the term *no fixed abode*)
To somewhere with a less exclusive code?
Would they exchange their privacy for loud

Car alarms ringing almost every night?
For now they stand where no one steals a car.
Would they be safer staying where they are,
Wiser, as well? Too wise to move too far?
You think they would. You think you know you're right.

Altering the Angle

Quick, summon up your out-of-bed persona;
Start acting like you met me at a conference
Ages ago. Throw in a bit of indifference.
This month's adventure stars the cowboy loner,
And, look, it's almost time to do something spontaneous.

For all your talk of changes and the future
You wouldn't dream of altering the angle
Of your ponytail, relinquishing the single
Newspaper life. Under that cloak of culture
Your past consumes your present like a vulture.

I'm flexible, but why should I adapt
To being systematically ignored
By somebody whose scores don't make the board?
And as for warmth you might as well be wrapped
In clingfilm on an isolation ward.

Proud of how unemotional you are,
You coast along – never a peak or trough –
And I'm your novelty inside a jar;
You count the seconds of my wearing off,
Talk about how you'd like to travel far
Away from me. I hope the sea is rough.

So, what's the next meticulously planned
Escapade going to be? Will you expand
Your consciousness, experiment with lust,
Make a few notes and think you've got it sussed,
The science of excitement in your hand?

Well, here's goodbye. Experiment with that.
You're far too big a space for me to fill,
And even with the greatest strength of will
I can't hallucinate a rolling hill
On land that is predominantly flat.

When He's at Home

A patch provokes the lazy eye,
Pillars support the dome.
I say his name and friends reply
Who's he when he's at home?

He's a performing art on stage.
At work he's smart and busy.
He's Times New Roman on the page.
When he's at home, who is he?

He's the road atlas man in cars.
On fairground rides he's dizzy.
He's wet in rain and drunk in bars.
When he's at home, who is he,

When there is nothing that provokes
And when there's no support?
Nothing. The show is over, folks,
And sooner than I thought.

Slow Start, Weak End

Dirty. That's what you think and how you smell.
Slow start, weak end, and now the late, deluded
Head of the fan club rings a tarnished bell.
Don't wonder what went wrong. That's easy – you did.
You're smiling at me now. What's the occasion?
I watch you as you go into remission.
My touch is more and more of an abrasion
And we will never find the right position.
Nothing rubs off on me; I take a shower
Mainly because there's nowhere else to hide.
If you have good points, princes in the tower
Is all they are. You keep them shut inside.
I need a break. You know the kind I mean:
Like the weekend. Like disinfectant. Clean.

Two Sonnets

DARLING SWEATHEART

He couldn't spell. The letters were addressed
to *Darling Sweatheart*, though he acted mean
when I was with him. Probably the best
present he gave me was some margarine –

a tub of Stork, half full. It wasn't wrapped.
He shrugged and said *You might as well have this*.
He'd find excuses, say his lips were chapped
in an attempt to dodge my weekly kiss.

He'd made a comprehensive wedding plan
involving just the two of us. No way
were guests allowed. His dog would be Best Man.
I dithered. *What a life* he used to say,

Let's have a kid. If we get skint, we'll sell it.
He wasn't bad. It's just the way I tell it.

CREDIT FOR THE CARD

She took the credit for the card I sent.
It's bad enough that you are hers, not mine.
How dare she, after all the time I spent
Choosing and writing out your Valentine,
Pretend it came from her, after the date
And its significance had slipped her mind?
She saw her chance before it was too late
And claimed my card – mysterious, unsigned –
Became the face behind my question mark.
Now there's too much at stake. She can't confess.
She has conspired to keep you in the dark
Which fact, she knows, would make you like her less.
Her lips are sealed. She lied and she forgot
Valentine's Day. I didn't. Mine are not.

Fair to Say

It's fair to say you own a boat. It's yours.
Nothing luxurious. A rowing boat.
First it springs holes and then you lose the oars.
It's when the thing can barely stay afloat
Let alone speed you off to foreign shores –
At that point you no longer have a boat.

You rent a flat, a corrugated box,
No fancy furnishings, no welcome mat.
One day the landlord changes all the locks.
A dog moves in. It tries to kill your cat.
It's when the door stays closed, despite your knocks –
At that point you no longer have a flat.

You've got a boss. You've worked for him for years.
He is a firm, authoritative boss
Until one day the office disappears.
You ask him what to do. He's at a loss.
He looks away and covers up his ears –
At that point you no longer have a boss.

As for your man, the things he used to do
Like smile and speak, watch movies, make a plan,
Listen to music, kiss – to name a few –
He's given up, as if some kind of ban
Were on them all. When somebody who blew
Hot now blows cold and you've done all you can –
At that point you no longer have a man.

When his turned back makes one bed feel like two –
At that point you no longer have a clue.

The During Months

Like summer in some countries and like rain
in mine, for nuns like God, for drunks like beer,
like food for chefs, for invalids like pain,
you've occupied a large part of the year.

The during months to those before and since
would make a ratio of ten to two,
counting the ones spent trying to convince
myself there was a beating heart in you

when diagrams were all you'd let me see.
Hearts should be made of either blood or stone,
or both, like mine. There's still December free –
the month in which I'll save this year, alone.

Three Poems about Cars and Driving

IN THE BLIND SPOT

I check the rearview mirror. Has she seen us?
And is that *her* face in the car behind?
And does she stare from Polos and Cortinas,
Or is it guilt that's playing with my mind?
And if so, why? It's not as though I've chucked her.
This lesson hardly constitutes a breach
Of trust. I'm only with this new instructor
While she is unavailable to teach.
But still, I should have said, I should have told her.
Is that her car, about to overtake,
Or in the blind spot, just behind my shoulder?
In all three mirrors as I hit the brake?
And while I fight these visions, how the hell
Am I supposed to learn to drive as well?

SLOW IT RIGHT DOWN

Nobody gets priority with you
So all concerned must do the best they can:
Be safe and stop, be brave and charge on through –
You are an unmarked crossroads of a man.

Some men I know are double yellow lines
Or traffic lights for everyone to see.
I'm practised when it comes to give way signs
But unmarked crossroads are a mystery

And this time I shall do it by the book,
Slow it right down and read my highway code;
Before reversing, take one final look –
An unmarked crossroads down an unknown road.

FOR B440 UBU

On the horizon there's a car.
I do not often look that far
But for my postman's car I do,
For B440 UBU.

Until the postman comes, I wait.
It regularly makes me late,
This waiting for a distant view
Of B440 UBU.

My boyfriend tries to make me leave
The house, refuses to believe
I've seen the shape, the size, the hue
Of B440 UBU.

He says the car's too far away.
He adds that if I'm wrong, I may
Be waiting here an hour or two
For B440 UBU.

I tell him I can see that far.
I recognise my postman's car.
I know that what I say is true –
That's B440 UBU.

The Learner

Your only hope of knowing how he feels
is wading through the electronic mail.
He'll walk away with feet like cutting wheels,
turning the ground on which you stand to shale
        when his heart peels
off, like a stick-on L-plate in a heavy gale.

This man believes in dragons breathing fire.
When he stands still, you'll hear his shaking bones
and when he moves he's like a rolling tyre
over a box of semi-precious stones,
        faster and higher
than L-plates loose in twenty-mile-an-hour zones.

Be careful of the drinks he wants to buy
if he does not at first appear thick skinned.
Soon as you tell yourself he's scared or shy
he'll be the board where all your hopes are pinned.
        Then watch him fly
off, like a truant L-plate carried by the wind.

The Treasurer

He's much too busy to appreciate
my effort in his clean and perfect pages.
I watch him work himself into a state
over this year's accounts, the rise in wages,
and see it in his face each time we speak –
not worth an extra twenty-seven pounds a week.

I tell him that he's under too much stress
and ought to let me do another day.
He shakes his head because it costs him less,
wanting my time but not enough to pay
for more of it, and who am I to gripe?
Plenty of people can stuff envelopes and type.

How can I tell him that I'd work for free
just for the chance to touch his winter coat?
Some treasurer. He doesn't treasure me.
I wonder how the business stays afloat,
for he must lack investment sense, my boss,
running his greatest asset at so great a loss.

Lusting after Walter Knife

They mention him without intent
And you pretend you haven't heard
Anything more than what was meant
Because his name's a household word.

Imagine – loving Peter Chair
Would make deciding where to sit
Almost impossible to bear
If you connected him with it,

Or lusting after Walter Knife –
One move to spread your margarine
Might make you want to stab his wife;
Not what things are but what they mean

To you, so dig a hole and hide
Unless his name is Pete or Loam
And if the man's called Mountainside
You might be better off at home.

To Whom it May Concern at the Whalley Range Driving Test Centre

Please don't regard this as a threat.
We'll be the best of friends, I bet,
Though up to now we've never met
And I'd just like the chance to get
Some feelings off my chest,

Which won't take very long to read.
The point is this: I must succeed.
I'll never drink and drive or speed.
I really want and really need
To pass my driving test,

And, well, if God forbid I fail
I'll stand outside your house and wail,
Circle your place of work and trail
Black L-plates from a black gauze veil.
I'll be the petrol guest

At every gathering you host,
Proposing a malignant toast,
A sickly, seatbelt-wearing ghost,
Liking you least instead of most.
I'll never let you rest

And may your Fiat Tipo burn.
Sorry. That sounds a little stern.
My nerves are bad. Tonight I learn
Left hand reverse and three point turn
So wish me all the best.

The Pros and the Cons

He'll be pleased if I phone to ask him how he is.
It will make me look considerate and he likes considerate people.

He'll be reassured to see that I haven't lost interest,
which might make him happy and then I'll have done him a favour.

If I phone him right now I'll get to speak to him sooner
than I will if I sit around waiting for him to phone me.

He might not want to phone me from work in case someone hears
    him
and begins (or continues) to suspect that there's something
    between us.

If I want to and don't, aren't I being a bit immature?
We're both adults. Does it matter, with adults, who makes the
    first move?

But there's always the chance he'll back off if I come on too strong.
The less keen I appear, the more keen he's likely to be,

and I phoned him twice on Thursday and once on Friday.
He must therefore be fully aware that it's his turn, not mine.

If I make it too easy for him he'll assume I'm too easy,
while if I make no effort, that leaves him with more of a challenge.

I should demonstrate that I have a sense of proportion.
His work must come first for a while and I shouldn't mind waiting.

For all I know he could have gone off me already
and if I don't phone I can always say, later, that I went off him first.

Into His Plans

The truth, which on my more possessive days
Lurks in the background, spoiling all the fun,
That I am not the only game he plays,
Neither am I the most important one,
I've always known. I knew before I fell
Into his plans. I knew because he said,
And, flattered that he wanted me as well,
I didn't wish he wanted me instead
At that stage. Now I'm feeling discontent
And longing for a more familiar mess –
Having been many people's main event,
People who've hurt me more and liked me less
Than he does – also knowing that it's wrong
To think this way, not thinking it for long.

On the Silver Side

However you may be under a different bridge,
under this one you're luminous and round,
watch-faced or moon-faced, split, on the silver side,
glowing right through me as I begin sprouting wires.

I have looked for you under the bridge of the curling stones,
under the oily bridge and under the fence
that believes it's a bridge. You aren't under any of those,
however you may be under a different bridge,

one made of shells and crowns and packs of cards,
coliseums and changing rooms, but you'd better not be
under my bridge wishing you were somewhere else.
However you may be under a different bridge.

Preventative Elegy

There will not be a burial,
There will not be a wake.
No ashes will be sprinkled
Over the stream or lake.
There won't be a cremation
A coffin or a shroud.
No hearse will park along the road –
Your death is not allowed.

There will not be a graveyard,
There'll be no marble stone
Bearing a carved endearment.
No flesh will shrink to bone
And in the town that loves you
There'll be no sobbing crowd.
No one inherits anything –
Your death is not allowed.

No grief will need to be disguised
As just a bit upset.
No one will wonder whether to
Remember or forget
Or which would cause the greater pain,
And whether we laughed or rowed
Last time will be irrelevant –
Your death is not allowed.

Others will die instead of you.
A fixed amount must die
(If there are quotas with these things)
And strangers' wives will cry
But I will have no need to say
I loved you and was proud
To be what I have been to you –
Your death is not allowed.

Person Specification

The ideal candidate for the position
of soulmate to the all-important you
should say she loves you, of her own volition,
every five minutes, and it should be true.

She must be motivated and ambitious
but feminine. She will be good at art,
at homely things. Her meals should be nutritious.
The ideal candidate will win your heart

with her prowess in bed. She will look stunning
in public, turn at least ten heads per day.
She should do most of (if not all) the running
and be prepared for marriage straight away.

Points will be lost for boring occupations,
excessive mood swings, drugs and other men.
To those who fail, your deep commiserations.
This post will not be advertised again.

The Sight of Mares

Either a dark horse, not a horse at all,
or else a horse resentful of the label,
at giddy-ups he turns to face the wall.
He says he's never been inside a stable.

I take his word for it (he ought to know),
but others disagree and say he moves
just like a horse. Explain, then, why he's so
uncomfortable with the idea of hooves

and why he shudders at the sight of mares
and all the other things you can't explain.
Four legs he may have – so do beds and chairs,
but something makes you call his hair a mane

and you imagine he must have a tail
though you would never say so to his face,
not when he puts his saddle up for sale
and says he hasn't heard about the race

in which all horses should be taking part.
He seems sincere, but bear in mind, of course,
even if he is not a horse at heart
that doesn't mean he's not, in fact, a horse,

though given all the medals he could win
being a horse, it's odd that he would choose
not to be one. You ought to see him grin
when he pulls off his semi-circle shoes.

Glass Eyebrow

the end   an eyebrow   where I draw the line
glass eyebrow   I occasionally raise
for company   only the Shugborough sign
only an eyebrow misses you   bouquets

The Shugborough sign has seen me go South East,
has seen me head South West and to the coast.
The Shugborough sign has seen me as the least
important person, seen me as the most
and on some trips I turn to it and boast.

the end an eyebrow where I draw the line

Some people never see the Shugborough sign.
They pass it half asleep or in a daze.
No one has claimed it so it must be mine
glass eyebrow I occasionally raise
glass eyebrows on selected motorways.

Drivers have hurtled past the white and brown
Shugborough sign and passengers have dozed,
while I have passed the A-road to your town,
many a time, pretending it was closed

or not a possibility   my head
that it went wrong   for which I do not blame
the motorways   for even though they led
to you   may lead to better things   the same

Negotiate the fairest deal you can
although it might mean pulling punks from trees.
Those of us searching for a Shugborough man
request a motorway extension, please.

So bless so bless the Shugborough sign and praise
even the signs you may not understand.
You see them by the sides of motorways
but can't imagine what they might have planned:

a parrot as a substitute for words,
a festival assistant with a sneer
fluttering slowly to a world of birds.
The Shugborough man has missed another year,

but he is coming just as you were not,
and meanwhile life goes on and plastic trays
bring all-day brunches and the weather's hot

only an eyebrow misses you   bouquets

Four Short Poems

THE MIND I LOSE

Whether the things I feel are true
or just illusion on my part,
I think that I'm in love with you
and wouldn't want to doubt my heart.

You say my heart may not exist.
I know it does, but isn't what
I once believed. This adds a twist,
the like of which can save a plot.

Feelings and thoughts are kept apart
unfairly by the words we choose.
Find me a better name than heart
by which to call the mind I lose.

BREAK THE COMPASS

To love him would be inconvenient.
My helpful friends are making out a list
of how my spare time might be better spent,
ironing clothes and towels – I get the gist,
but if he needs a pen-knife or a tent
that I can put discreetly in his hands,
if I'm the only one who can prevent
the dereliction of his little lands
then I will strike the talking oblongs dumb
and break the compass if they try to steer
my thoughts away from him, and they'll become
the inconvenience they claim to fear.

TO WISH ON YOU

You left a yellow imprint on my eye
which I'll remember longer than your face.
In a dark room with roof like winter sky
you were the only star to light the place.

You stood beneath the spotlight and you shone
while its strong beams fell down on you and then
you stepped away and all the shine was gone.
I'm waiting here for you to shine again.

Convince this audience that you belong
up there in dark or light and I will try
to wish on you but only for as long
as there's a yellow imprint on my eye.

FIND HIM GONE

Somebody else is sitting in your chair,
doing the same thing you did, just the same,
except he isn't you. His build, his hair –
both lighter, and he has a longer name

so now the wages book looks different, signed.
His tapes are where your bike-lights used to be,
next to the floppy disc tray, just behind
your mug (now his) which still says *I love tea*.

He doesn't though. Sometimes I catch his eye
and wonder if I'll find him gone one day
or if he'll see a different face at my
desk in due course. But he just looks away.

She Can Win Favour

Her friend the locksmith readily believes
the tales she tells of all the locks she's picked.
She can win favour with a gang of thieves
by itemising all the goods she's nicked,
and then you hear her talking to a judge
about the many crimes she has prevented.
Confectioners are told she's fond of fudge,
landlords, about the properties she's rented.
She can be just like anyone she meets
by flicking through her catalogue of poses –
ally of underdogs and of élites,
to gardeners she boasts of pruning roses,
to firemen of the time she braved the fire –
never to liars, though, that she's a liar.

Ms Quicksand is a Bitch

Reflected personality –
defence and favoured myth
of Mrs Smith, whose treachery
is loved by Mr Smith.

Husband is nice so wife must be
when right beside the moans
of Mrs Jones, what do you see?
The smile of Mr Jones.

Mrs Brown's shoes have heavy soles
for treading people down
while badgers, dolphins, bears and moles
are saved by Mr Brown.

When Mrs House (née Flat) agreed
to marry Mr House
she must have known that she would need
a mitigating spouse

but would he live with, sleep with, stay
with, would he share a bed . . . ?
Yes, and you see it every day,
the wed, the not yet wed –

If mountaintops were not too high
to recognise a ditch,
then Mr Hill would not deny
Ms Quicksand is a bitch.

Running into Late

Where is the taxi's plastic pyramid?
Wasting another evening in the shed.
The case you carry never does or did
succeed in putting motives in your head.
Nobody has enough of anything,
nor will they find it underneath the lid
of some enamelled box, coiled in a spring

in the settee that festers on the ranch,
which was where I used to balance my peanut butter,
or in the tree you study branch by branch
or in the stadium or in the gutter.
You talk of nature and the man-made world
but miss the boot-sale and the avalanche.
Hair that alternately is crimped and curled

(if hair is not enough, what hope has skin?)
has not been known to drag you from the screen,
and is your bottle really worth the spin
if punts and parents jointly intervene?
Is God distinguished from the latest cult?
Not if you run your life by maximin:
aim for the least obnoxious worst result.

My main objection isn't that you wait
but that impatience would achieve far more.
If early wasn't running into late
I could respect the things you waited for.
Meanwhile I must conclude you're not the one,
watching you lift the packing from the crate,
looking for relics of ancestral fun.

The Downfall of Her Oscillating Head

After he called her idol nondescript
both what she felt and who she felt it for
became a pool of oil from which she slipped
into a strange illusion of the law.

On paper headed *this peculiar thing*,
the summons that he found beside his bed
charged him with rigid air conditioning,
the downfall of her oscillating head.

With strictly rehabilitative zest
all traces of him vanished from the lease
to relocate, entirely for the best,
on a mosaic patio in Greece

where his bread rolls were filled with Feta cheese
and round machines on rubber tubes inhaled
the insects from his bath – how to appease
spikes on which one was recently impaled.

Back home, the sensors he installed detect
that she is eating popcorn by the fire,
wondering how a sane man can respect
the form above the content of desire.

He leaves his business card on several boats.
His name is linked to some obscure mistake
while, in a jogging suit, the idol floats
off in a wicker basket down the lake

and doesn't ring but makes the same joke twice
about the things he hasn't done for years.
His fading mouth declares it might be nice.
Lords are behind it when he disappears.

Two Poems about Music

These poems were commissioned for the 1995 Huddersfield Contemporary Music Festival

HER KIND OF MUSIC

Her kind of music was a song
About a broken heart,
While his was complicated, long,
And labelled 'modern art'

With links to the chromatic scale.
The opera he wrote,
To her ears, was a lengthy wail
Upon a single note.

She struggled to acquire his taste
(As frequently occurs),
While, with enthusiastic haste,
He did away with hers.

WHEN A POET LOVES A COMPOSER

One look at him and I forgot,
Embarrassingly soon,
That music ought to have, if not
Lyrics, at least a tune.

He's highbrow in a big, big way
But when he sees that I'm
The one, he'll think that it's okay
For poetry to rhyme.

Soft-Handed Man

She couldn't love a man who had soft hands
and didn't do constructive things with wood,
but if she met one that she loved, she could.
She's right to say we all make strange demands
and right to think that no one understands.
Hard hands are not indicative of good

character, don't infallibly belong
to rugged, silent types who rarely shave,
who are, in equal measures, kind and brave.
Just over the horizon there's a strong
soft-handed man waiting to prove her wrong,
and when a person proves you wrong, they save

acres of mind you were about to close
and turn it into habitable land.
Each time you hold an unexpected hand
and stare at features that you never chose,
you're dealing with authority that knows
better than you how well things can be planned.

Selling His Soul

When someone says they have a poet's soul
You can imagine laughing in their face –
A sensible reaction on the whole
But he convinced me that it was the case
And that his poet's soul was out of place
What with his body selling advertising space.

The easy explanations sprang to mind –
Was he pretentious, arrogant, insane,
Or was it possible he'd been assigned
Just what he said, and that his poet's brain,
Like a Laguna in the left hand lane,
Found itself trapped on unfamiliar terrain?

Even if there was just a one-in-five
Chance of it being true, I'd take the bet;
The souls of advertising salesmen thrive
In many of the poets I have met,
And if I'm right to think I won't forget
His soul, he's passed the best test anyone could set.

His life was going to change. He felt inspired,
He said, and vanished from my line of sight.
I didn't follow him. I have admired
The way Lagunas fly past on the right
While slower cars can only watch their flight,
Stuck in a ten mile tailback, every foggy night.

Double That Amount

for my car

It's not the money I will have to pay
To Nixon's Garage for the odd new part –
I would put double that amount their way
If they could beat the panels of my heart
Back to their happy shape before the dent
To your rear door. That would be cash well spent.

Now all my friends are trying to explain
What, in the land of logic, may be true:
That cars don't suffer. Cars do not feel pain.
I believe this like most car owners do
Yet can imagine how you're going to feel
For all the time it takes your door to heal.

This time next week, you'll be as good as new
But time is not the comfort that we need
Since I can wish it forwards (backwards too)
But can't change its direction or its speed,
Can't flip to either after or before
The damage to your injured, dented door.

As good as new, though – that means nothing lost
Apart from money, more of which I'll make
And your repairs, however much they cost
Are cheap to me. Money for money's sake
Is worthless in my mind, where feelings count
For everything and double that amount.

Ticket to Staines

I'd emerged from the second of two freezing trains
With a bag full of cheese salad sandwich remains
When I met a tree surgeon who said he was broke
And asked me to buy him a ticket to Staines.

He told me a jumbled, unfortunate tale
About how he had broken the terms of his bail
And he had to get back to his Mum's before ten
Or the cops would be taking him straight back to jail.

He told me his story outside Euston station
Describing his crime and its justification:
His tree surgeon's chainsaw had sliced through a train
In an effort to sabotage veal transportation.

His Mum had lumbago and no credit card
For a telephone booking. I thought long and hard
And it seemed to be me and me only that stood
Between him and a grilling at New Scotland Yard.

With diminishing faith in the state of my brains
And without quite condoning the slicing of trains
I led him past Knickerbox, Sock Shop and all
And bought that tree surgeon a ticket to Staines.

What will become of him? Where will he go?
(And don't say, 'You paid for it, you ought to know.')
I mean, is there a place for him? Is there a place
For a lawbreaking tree surgeon, chainsaw in tow?

There's a place for the tyrant who rules and constrains,
For the person who keeps other people in chains.
Wherever that tree surgeon goes, freedom reigns.
I wish I could see him arriving in Staines.

Postcard from a Travel Snob

I do not wish that anyone were here.
This place is not a holiday resort
with karaoke nights and pints of beer
for drunken tourist types – perish the thought.

This is a peaceful place, untouched by man –
not like your seaside-town-consumer-hell.
I'm sleeping in a local farmer's van –
it's great. There's not a guest house or hotel

within a hundred miles. Nobody speaks
English (apart from me and rest assured,
I'm not your sun-and-sangria-two-weeks
small-minded-package-philistine-abroad).

When you're as multi-cultural as me,
your friends become wine connoisseurs, not drunks.
I'm not a British tourist in the sea;
I am an anthropologist in trunks.

His Rising

They say it started with the climbing frame
his parents bought him when he was a boy.
They say that he was never quite the same,
that he progressed from climbing frame to trees,
            wanting a bigger toy.
They say now there is nothing that he sees,
nothing protruding that he won't ascend.
When he looks down, people the size of fleas
seem unimpressive from his higher perch;
            to recognise a friend
would mean binoculars, a pointless search.
His bride-to-be, a tiny dot below,
whom he would marry just to climb the church,
can stare up pipes until her neck is sore
            but she will never know
who or what kept him on the ground before,
what he now feels the need to rise above.
They say the only way we can endure
his rising and resist the urge to sink
            is with our minds off love.
Our mode of elevation is to think
about the closeness needed for a war.

Loss Adjuster

Scale down your expectations once again
from rest of life to years to one whole night
to will he wander past a phone or pen.
If he would only either ring or write.
Get real and scale those expectations down
from conversation to a single word –
seen through the window of a shop in town
if not by you then by a trusted third
party, or, if a sighting is too much
to hope for (as undoubtedly it is)
scale down your hopes and aim to see or touch
someone whose name sounds similar to his.
A scale of one to ten. Two weeks ago
he dared to keep you waiting while he slept.
Scale down much further and today's poor show
tomorrow you'll be happy to accept.

Two Hundred and Sixty-Five Words

I know exactly what I want to say.
I've estimated how long it will take.
I've weighed the trouble that will come my way
Against the difference saying it could make
And with no help from the mysterious They
Who ought to fight for people's right to speak,
I use my word allowance for today,
My conversation ration for the week

To talk about the baby with no manger,
The gold, myrrh, frankincense he never got,
Who was brought up for profit by a stranger
And invoiced for a rattle and a cot.
His rattle was the one thing he was fond of.
No time to say what matters most to me
Before I'm heard, before they snap the wand of
The upstart fairy on the Christmas tree.

She over-waved that wand. She used to wave it
At all bad things, hoping to make them good.
Who confiscated it? Who, later, gave it
Back to her as a heap of broken wood?
Call now with some inane response or other.
There are two phones, a black one and a white.
The right one will connect you with your brother;
The wrong one and your brother died last night.

Soon I might say *Ninety-five pounds. Nice weather*,
And call you by a name that's not your own.
You think they might put two and two together.
Sound old, sound boring and hang up the phone.
You think if we speak out then they can't touch us,
The Indiscriminately-Known-As-They
Who are responsible. Well, in as much as
I'm one of them, wave all your wands this way.

I'll Give Him This

The clothes he irons either burn or drown
And he wears tennis shoes to scale a cliff.
I doubt that he could name two shops in town
But he can tell a Rizla from a riff.
I'll give him this: the man can really roll a spliff.

He fears asparagus and foods with shells.
He can make heavy inroads overnight
Into your stock of Boddingtons and Bells.
That's a great song, he'll say, and he'll be right,
Rolling a spliff that's not too loose and not too tight.

He wouldn't know a saucer from a cup
But he can talk about election polls
While strumming his guitar or skinning up.
He loses small things like remote controls
But find fault with the songs he loves, the joints he rolls.

He's never dabbled in nouvelle cuisine
Or dazzled with a literary joke.
Don't tell me how inadequate he's been
At parties; if the guests don't sing or smoke,
If it's some vol-au-vent affair, he's not your bloke

But if you like tobacco on your rug
And if you want to watch a work of art
Emerging from a soft, illegal drug
His resurrection brain, his cowboy heart
Are highly recommended as a place to start.

My Enemies

My enemies, polished inside their caskets
My enemies sparkle behind glass doors
My enemies, curled into tilted baskets
My enemies, not yours

my enemies   You cannot steal or hire them
my enemies   You cannot loan or share
my enemies   Don't tidy or admire them
Don't even see them there

my enemies   Steer clear of the display case
My enemies try to make false amends
my enemies   The pallor of your grey face
will make them shine like friends

My enemies, proud of their faults and failings
my enemies   You take them out for tea
My enemies, beckoning through the railings
at a novice enemy

My enemies will give you proper training
My enemies shuffle up shelves for you
my enemies   The old ones are complaining
I like them better new

my   a new enemy   an equidistant
enemy showing every friend the door
politely, like a personal assistant
my enemies   One more

The Subject and the Object

Where injuries undress behind a screen
there is a way round saying what you mean.
The most decisive firebomb will assume
           the profile of a
ladder at the window of a burning room.

No sooner is your loft secured with string –
listen – the cellar crowns another King
with whom there is no time to disagree,
           so subtle that he
spells the word revenge without the letter 'v',

in deference to whom fish take the bones
out of themselves. Peaches emit their stones.
This King is an unusual event.
           You'd think a cat was
purring when his subjects came to pay the rent.

I'll give up words like 'troublesome' and 'hard'
and buy some skin cream for his business card.
One half that calculates, one half that cares –
           our combination
King, the best thing we have ever had downstairs,

attributing the days he saves to Spring,
and to the wind the tearing off of string.
He takes no credit and his voice is soft
           when he assures you
all you hear is cries of birds above the loft.

What You Deserve

I could pay you a fortune;
alternatively
I could ask for a fortune
and you could pay me.

I could tell you true stories
and false ones as well
but they all would be stories
I'd rather not tell.

I can live without justice,
at least live without
any version of justice
I might bring about,

for if my contribution
was wounds in the fight
shouldn't your contribution
be putting it right?

I have built no defences
nor will I attack
someone else's defences;
I'll get my own back

without blackmail or violence,
which call for less nerve
than to wait in long silence
for what you deserve.

All Wrong for Some

The cutlery is starting to annoy you.
It's either ladles or it's slotted spoons.
Early and late conspire to destroy you.
If it's not mornings then it's afternoons.
Both are containers clearly marked *conniption*.
Both are sufficient cause to be irate.
Mornings are not part of your job description,
Neither are afternoons. Early and late –
The way they start apart, then club together
To form a day, the way those footsteps crunch
Along the gravel path, along your tether
Right to the end. You blame it all on lunch,
For linking what should not be linked, for spawning
An afternoon as worthless as the morning.

You spend it looking forward to it ending
But when it ends, something is still not right:
You realise you can't go on pretending
That day is more unpopular than night
Or Winter more unpopular than Summer.
You blame the Springs and Autumns in between.
Boring old season, seasonal newcomer –
Neither is green enough, both are too green.
Enough to turn your masterpiece to stencils.
You wave your paintbrush at the scary face.
Paint starts to run. If you had stuck to pencils
That grey self-portrait would have known its place.
Now, when you look at it inside its frame, you
See that you hate yourself, and who can blame you.

Nod and Smile

'You couldn't take him anywhere,' she said,
'Even your best friends wouldn't want to know.'
She must have thought I harboured in my head
A glossy guide to places we could go.

'There's nowhere I could take him,' I agree.
She takes the opportunity to breathe a
Sigh of relief, then she turns back to me
And says, 'He'd never let you leave him either.'

'I couldn't ever leave him,' I concede.
There's much agreement in our brief exchange.
She's thrilled and I am not, but we're agreed
That circumstances won't improve or change,

That I could save myself a lot of pain.
There's not a word she says I don't believe –
Much easier only to entertain
Thoughts of a person you can take, or leave.

Pink and the Gang

Pink house in a grey town,
Thin house on a long street,
White stone house and brown –
All raise their rents to beat

The house that won't compete –
The tall house by the sea
Who says, to cries of cheat,
Do not charge rent for me.

However loud his voice
They'll make their rents as large.
They will be seen as choice;
He, as ashamed to charge.

White, brown, pink and thin
Monopolise the streets.
Materialists move in,
Are rewarded with receipts

While the tall sea house takes
Nothing but love and thanks
From his tenant, who mistakes
Pink and the gang for banks.

The Man Who Wouldn't Share His Garden
with a Wolf

I try to keep my cool –
difficult when the thieving
bastard has got his paws inside my pool,
tail on my grass, and shows no sign of leaving.
I don't know what the fool
thinks he's achieving.

He calls himself my friend.
The place, he calls exquisite.
Creep. Just a while, he said. So, to extend
that while to permanence is friendly, is it?
A visit with no end
is not a visit.

Which would be more unkind,
to draw a line, restrict him
to one half of the garden, or to find
a pretext upon which I could evict him?
To have him off my mind,
even inflict him

on somebody I hate –
one of the grin and bear it
brigade, who almost pushed him through my gate,
who now sit back and murmur how unfair it
is for a man of great
wealth not to share it.

Good guilt-inducing trick,
but false, since I would harden
my heart, if I was poor, over a brick.
You heard me. Never mind I beg your pardon.
Get the ungrateful prick
out of my garden.

Liberation Day

My tunnel wasn't yet complete.
I shook from heavy earrings
New dust each day around my feet
In muddy forest clearings.

The aperture was well concealed,
My tools were safe and polished
When a news bulletin revealed
Walls were to be demolished.

I have shed large amounts of sweat,
I've crawled and cried and shivered
And now I hear we're going to get
Deliverance delivered.

I am not over-keen to bleed,
I didn't take to scraping
But it is one thing being freed,
Another thing escaping.

Digging has helped me through the day,
Digging has made me stronger.
I can't, with nothing in the way,
Make my short tunnel longer.

I will sit centre stage, front row
And clap as each brick tumbles
But where will my half-tunnel go
If the whole building crumbles?

I'll wait for Liberation Day.
The roof will lift, the sun'll
shine and with new, free speech I'll say
I want to build my tunnel.

In Layman's Terms

If he wants proof, he only has to ask.
Let him admit to disbelief and doubt.
Tell him that I am equal to the task
Of driving all his reservations out
And if he sees no face behind the mask,
Where is the faith I've heard so much about?

If he wants proof, he had his proof before.
I could provide a bibliography.
He doesn't think I know him anymore;
I've mixed him up with what he used to be.
I also may have changed and yet he's sure
That he addresses his remarks to me.

Our words connect the present to the past
Each time we speak, simply by making sense.
So tell him this, the next time doubt is cast:
The risks I take are at my own expense.
If he has faith then he should be the last
To give up hope, despite the evidence;

A standpoint known as love, in layman's terms,
Namely determination to succeed
Though odds are stacked and though suspicion worms
Its way through hearts and nothing's guaranteed.
No fact disproves all this and none confirms
And if he still needs proof, he'll have to need.

The Good Loser

I have portrayed temptation as amusing.
Now he can either waver or abstain.
His is a superior kind of losing
And mine is an inferior brand of gain.

His sacrifice, his self-imposed restriction
Will get through this controversy intact
For his is a superior kind of fiction
And mine is an inferior brand of fact.

I have displayed my most attractive feature
And he his least, yet still the match seems odd.
For I am a superior kind of creature
And he is an inferior brand of god

And if he cuts me off without a warning
His is the book from which I'll take a leaf
For his is a superior kind of mourning
And ours a most inferior brand of grief.

A Strong Black Coffee for the Sleeping Dog

They let you in. You interrupt their dinner.
You're on your back instead of on your knees.
If you behave yourself, one day you'll win a
Glimpse of your loved one's chips and mushy peas.
　　　　What do I have to do to be a sinner?
　　　　Turn a saint's pencil forty-five degrees.

He had a small square yard for us to smoke in,
Behind a hut and safe from parish spies.
The room his parents used to put strange folk in
Was also square and of a matching size.
　　　　I listened to the same twelve songs and spoke in
　　　　The hushed tones of a consolation prize.

Perhaps I wasn't any consolation.
Perhaps he didn't want to be consoled.
Years ago, when he had an explanation
And would have told me, I would not be told.
　　　　I hang around the graveyard and the station,
　　　　Outside the dog-eared college, feeling old,

And glamorise the benches and the matches.
I put the faces back inside the room.
His jacket with the shiny shoulder patches –
Does he still have it and, if not, to whom
　　　　Does it belong? One drops, another catches.
　　　　One has a spade and plenty to exhume.

By now you will be guessing my agenda,
That I am here for reasons of my own,
Not being shy or wise enough to send a
Token or two then leave you all alone.
　　　　I'm here in what should be my place, to spend a
　　　　Day with a gentleman I should have known.

Since neither of the heartless queens is present,
I have become a princess not a frog
As far as he's concerned, but what bland, pleasant
Creature might he be stalking through the fog?
        I've got a croissant shaped just like a crescent,
        A strong black coffee for the sleeping dog.

I've come to demonstrate that to be able
Is what counts most. Too late and not too late
Have been defined today, and though unstable
Has given way to steady, mad to great,
        If he still keeps those objects on his table,
        There is a sort of chance, at any rate.

Sleep Well

He shook the feeling back into his arm
when its strange numbness woke him with a cry.
His wobbly leg caused only slight alarm
before connecting with its blood supply.

It's one thing, ladies, gentlemen, to wake
as did the man described above, like him
to feel dead digits, and to shake and shake
for a reunion with whichever limb

but in the early hours, with a start,
do not, like him, wake as an empty sack.
That man slept wrongly on his head and heart
and he will never get the feeling back.